SIGHTSEERS
ESSENTIAL TRAVEL GUIDES TO THE PAST

SHAKESPEARE'S

LONDON

A GUIDE TO THE TUDOR CITY
AND ITS THEATRES

JULIE FERRIS

KINGFISHER

KINGFISHER
Kingfisher Publications Plc
New Penderel House
283–288 High Holborn
London WC1V 7HZ

Written and edited by Julie Ferris
Senior Designer Jane Tassie

Consultant Nicholas Robins
Illustrations Inklink Firenze
Kevin Maddison

Editorial Assistant Katie Puckett
Research Prue Grice
DTP Co-ordinator Nicky Studdart
Production Controller Kelly Johnson
Picture Research Manager Jane Lambert
Proofreader Sheila Clewley
Indexer Sylvia Potter

First published by Kingfisher Publications Plc 2000
1 3 5 7 9 10 8 6 4 2

1TR/1199/WKT/AT(AT)/140MA

A CIP catalogue record for this book is available from
the British Library.

ISBN 0 7534 0410 9

Printed in
Hong Kong/China

Contents

Introducing London

I t is the ideal time to visit this lively, bustling city. Queen Elizabeth has reigned over England for 31 years, and this political stability has brought economic and cultural prosperity to the country. London has grown rapidly in size and is now an international centre of trade. It is also a very popular destination for travellers, with plenty of sights and entertainments on offer.

Queen Elizabeth has been nicknamed the "Virgin Queen" because she has never married. She is the daughter of Henry VIII and Anne Boleyn, and she became queen in 1558.

Sightseers' tip As well as visiting established tourist sights such as the Tower of London, St Paul's Cathedral and London Bridge, it is well worth spending time exploring the narrow, medieval streets with their overhanging, half-timbered houses.

England is now a Protestant country, and Queen Elizabeth is head of the Church.

Foreign visitors are not always treated well. Children sometimes shout insults at them.

The city wall runs around three sides of London. On the fourth side is the River Thames.

Elizabeth's reign has seen an increase in the number and variety of entertainments on offer in London. Popular amusements include dancing, music, bear-baiting, archery and football. The new theatres, situated on the south bank of the River Thames opposite the city, are also a major attraction for Londoners and visitors alike. Try to catch a play by the promising young playwright William Shakespeare. There are daily performances of his plays in the Globe theatre, which opened earlier this year.

The recently built Royal Exchange is the trading and banking heart of the city. Every day it is packed with merchants conducting their business.

Travelling around

Although it is one of the biggest cities in Europe, everything in London is in easy walking distance. However, the narrow streets and lanes are smelly and muddy and are always crowded with people, carts and horses. It is much more pleasant, and very often quicker, to travel to different parts of the city by boat on the River Thames.

Sightseers' tip Wherries are light rowing boats small enough to dart in and out of the river traffic. Seats are upholstered and many have awnings to protect passengers from rain.

Travel on horseback if you are planning to venture out of the city. It is by far the speediest form of transport.

You can hire wherries (small river taxis) from one of the many landing places, or "river gates", along the riverside. To hail a wherryman, simply cry "Westward ho!" or "Eastward ho!", depending on the direction you wish to travel. You shouldn't have a long wait – there are usually plenty of wherrymen at the river gates, all eager for passengers. There is a standard penny fare for all wherry journeys.

If travelling out of London, you can stay overnight at one of the many wayside inns.

Traffic is increasingly becoming a problem in London and accidents are quite common.

Roads are in very poor condition, particularly outside the city. It can take a day to travel 40km.

Male visitors should think twice before travelling by coach – it is considered very unmanly to ride inside a carriage.

Recently introduced from Germany, the coach has become increasingly popular as a form of transport. However, the carriage does not have a suspension system so it is very uncomfortable to travel in, particularly over rough ground. However, it is covered over, and will protect passengers in bad weather.

7

What to wear

London is not the place for shrinking violets! Fashions are constantly changing and are often outrageous. Men wear doublets, breeches, stockings and short cloaks. Women wear elaborate gowns with wide skirts and stiff corsets. Many fashion trends, such as the distinctive ruff worn around the neck, have been greatly influenced by the royal court.

If you have plenty of spending money you will be able to buy garments made of satins, velvets and silks, and decorated with feathers and jewels. The poor, however, wear coarse, poorly fitting clothes.

Sightseers' tip

The starched linen ruffs worn around the neck may be very fashionable, but they are uncomfortable and restrict movement. Many people find it difficult to eat when wearing them.

The fashion of blacking out the front teeth has developed to disguise genuinely rotten teeth.

As well as scarlets and blues, fashion colours include gooseturd green and pease-porridge tawny.

The demand for wig hair means that children out alone may get their hair chopped off!

In England, as in other European countries, there are laws dictating who can wear what. The purpose of these laws is to make people lower in rank than nobles wear plainer clothes. Merchants, for example, are not allowed to wear certain expensive furs.

A pomander tied to the belt will help disguise unpleasant smells around the town.

You will need help getting dressed. Most garments have to be pinned, tied or laced together.

Trimmed beards and moustaches are considered *de rigueur* for gentlemen. Fashionable ladies usually wear their hair up. They paint their faces with white lead and vinegar and colour their lips bright red. Candle wax is smoothed onto the skin to disguise the pockmarks left by smallpox, but it tends to melt if the wearer stands too close to a fire!

As soon as they are out of baby clothes, children are dressed as young adults. Boys are dressed in the same clothes as girls until they are five years old, when they begin to wear breeches.

Food and drink

The quality and variety of food you eat during your visit to London will depend largely on your budget. If money is tight, you will have to make do with a basic diet of vegetables, bread and the occasional meat dish. If money is no object, be prepared for lavish banquets.

Meat such as venison and pheasant is hung in a store room for several days to improve the taste.

The Catholic custom of eating fish on Fridays still continues in Protestant England.

Too many sweet things and a lack of milk mean bad teeth are common.

Banquets can have as many as ten courses, but don't be daunted by the amount of food. It is the custom to eat only one or two mouthfuls of each course. Popular dishes include venison, mutton and swan, with fruit pies and jellies for sweets.

Although a few water pumps have been installed in the city, most people still rely on water-carriers. They sell water door-to-door and often wear a towel over their clothes to keep them dry.

Sightseers' tip

Most people have two big meals a day – at midday and in the early evening. The rich wash their food down with wine, while the poor drink ale.

Forks have only recently been introduced from Italy and are not in common use. Diners are usually provided with a napkin and spoon, but guests are sometimes expected to bring their own knife. It is polite to wash your hands before and after eating – particularly as you will often have to eat with your fingers.

Pewter pots and plates are popular, but also very costly. Some people rent their stock of pewter by the year.

Shopping

Why not commission a miniature portrait of yourself? It would make a great holiday souvenir!

London is a great place for shopping. Most streets are lined with shops and crowded with pedlars advertising their wares. You will, however, need to walk to different parts of the city to buy different goods. For example, vintners (wine merchants) can be found in Vintry Lane, and bakers are grouped together in Bread Lane and Pudding Lane.

Shopkeepers and their apprentices usually live in the same house as their business.

Booksellers in St Paul's churchyard sell copies of the latest plays, including Shakespeare's.

Watch out! Hanging signs are not always securely fixed and can sometimes fall down.

There are strict regulations for Tudor shopkeepers. Each trade has its own guild. No one can open a shop or practise a particular craft unless they have served a full apprenticeship of seven years, and paid an entrance fee to join the appropriate guild. The quality and price of goods are carefully controlled and monitored, and heavy fines are imposed on shopkeepers who use false weights and measures.

Hanging signs should indicate what a shop sells, but sometimes they are not changed when the shop changes hands. You may, for example, see a goldsmith's shop with a fishmonger's sign!

Sightseers' tip

Apprentices often call out to passers-by to encourage custom. However, you may be subjected to rude comments from an apprentice if you examine goods without buying them!

Accommodation

Accommodation will depend largely on your budget. If money is no object you will be able to stay in a fine, half-timbered Tudor town house with servants to attend to your needs. If this is not within your budget, you may find yourself in a slum house sharing a bed with several other people.

At midnight, night watchmen remind householders to lock their doors and douse fires.

If you're lucky enough to stay in the home of a wealthy Londoner, you will be impressed by the beautifully carved oak furniture. You should also get a good night's sleep – huge four-poster beds are a Tudor status symbol!

As well as soft pillows, mattress and warm coverlet, four-poster beds are hung with curtains to keep in the warmth at night.

The introduction of chimneys earlier this century has put an end to smoke-filled rooms.

 London has many rat-infested slums, particularly in the east end of the city.

 The inns on the roads out of London are very comfortable and have an excellent reputation.

Sightseers' tip ✔ Each storey of a Tudor house juts out over the floor below. There is such a small gap between the top stories of houses that they practically meet in the middle of the street.

Floors are covered with a layer of rushes. However, the rushes are often left unchanged for many months, and vermin, filth and bad smells are common. Perfumers are employed by householders to disguise bad odours.

The master of the house can relax in a comfortable oak chair with arm-rests. Other members of the household must make do with wooden stools.

The royal court has recently witnessed the introduction of a new sanitary device called the water closet. Unlike the chamber pot, this new invention uses water to flush away human waste. However, it is expensive and hasn't caught on yet.

The Globe theatre

William Shakespeare is the city's most popular playwright. He is a member of the theatre company based at the Globe, the Lord Chamberlain's Men.

No trip to London would be complete without a visit to one of the theatres on the south bank of the Thames. Although the first theatre was built only 23 years ago, plays have proved extremely popular, and thousands flock to the theatres every day. Entry to a performance costs one penny. You will have to pay another penny for a seat in the gallery.

Only men can be actors, so the female roles in plays are taken by boys.

Each theatre stages roughly 20 plays a year. Every new play has to be vetted by the Master of the Revels. He reports to the Lord Chamberlain and has the power to cut lines or even ban plays if he feels they are offensive or undermine authority.

The Globe theatre opened earlier this year. It is one of the largest in London and can hold up to 3,000 spectators. Watch out for cut-purses (thieves) who operate in the crowds during performances.

Fruit, cakes and drinks are sold by hawkers during performances.

 Make sure you wear warm clothes – theatres are open-air.

 You may need to hire a wherry to take you across the river to the theatres.

Sightseers' tip A raised flag indicates that there will be a performance. Plays are held in the afternoon and a trumpet is blasted three times to signal the start.

Fashionable London gentlemen pay for seats on the stage itself. They arrive late deliberately and delight in interrupting performances by coughing, yawning or calling out rude remarks. The rest of the audience can also be very rowdy, making the theatre an exciting place to visit.

Leisure time

There is no shortage of amusements to entertain the visitor to London. You can try your hand at some popular sports such as bowling, skittles, hockey, and football. Or, if you prefer a more relaxing time, many households enjoy musical evenings where everyone sings and plays musical instruments.

Londoners enjoy playing board games such as backgammon and chess.

London taverns are famous for the lively chatter and "merry wit" of their patrons. But they are also the scene of frequent brawls.

Blood-thirsty sports such as bull-baiting and bear-baiting are extremely popular. Fierce dogs are set on a tethered bear or bull, and bets are made on the outcome. Londoners also enjoy watching cock-fighting, and gamble large sums of money on which bird will win.

Sightseers' tip

Cock fights are held in Birdcage Walk and St-Giles-in-the-Fields. The cocks fight to the death, so it's not for the squeamish.

! Amusements do not go on late in the evening as the streets get very dark and crime is rife.

 There are archery shooting butts set up outside the city walls in the Moorfields.

The Lord Mayor's Show is held every year and includes a water pageant and a land procession.

Football is played using a leather ball. There are few rules. Two teams from different parts of the city meet between the two areas, and the object of the game is to get the ball back to your own part of the city any way you can. It is a very rough game and injuries are common.

The authorities frown upon the playing of football as it is a frequent cause of riot and bloodshed.

St Paul's Cathedral

Dominating the London skyline, St Paul's Cathedral marks the centre of the city, and is a must for sightseers. The huge, gothic cathedral is very much a part of city life. Londoners go there not only to worship and to hear sermons, but to conduct business and gossip.

Bibles in England are no longer written in Latin, and Catholic mass books have recently been replaced with English prayer books.

Religion has undergone many changes in the years since King Henry VIII declared himself head of the Church in place of the pope. These changes have been called the "Reformation". Under Queen Elizabeth, England is a Protestant, rather than a Roman Catholic, country.

There are laws requiring attendance at church on Sundays, but fines are rarely imposed.

Many tourists have left their mark by carving messages in St Paul's soft lead roof.

For a small price, the bellman allows children to climb the bell tower and drop things from the top!

If you are expecting the interior of St Paul's to be a peaceful, solemn place, prepare to be surprised! Londoners gather in the cathedral daily to exchange news and chat, show off new clothes, meet friends, do business and hire servants. It has even been known for cattle to be driven along the aisles as a short cut to the markets.

Sightseers' tip The cathedral's central aisle is known as "Paul's Walk". Every morning, it is crowded with people from all parts of London society, including cut-purses – so take care of your valuables.

Paul's Cross is an open-air pulpit in the cathedral's grounds. Sermons are preached here every Sunday.

St Paul's Cathedral originally had a 158-metre high steeple, but this burned down when it was struck by lightning in 1561.

Tower of London

In the east of the city is the famous Tower of London. It has a long and bloody history and is definitely worth a visit. As well as being a royal palace, the Tower is a prison, the only place in England where coins are minted, and home to the royal armoury, crown jewels and an animal menagerie.

Sightseers' tip

The Tower of London is very popular with sightseers. However, visitors wishing to see all its attractions should be prepared to tip officials generously.

The huge body armour of Henry VIII (Queen Elizabeth's father) is part of the impressive royal armoury held at the Tower.

Be careful not to offend or insult the queen during your stay, or you could enter the Tower as a prisoner through Traitor's Gate! Although high-ranking prisoners live in some comfort with their own servants, most people imprisoned in the Tower endure terrible, dank conditions, suffer cruel tortures and face eventual execution.

Two of Henry VIII's six wives were beheaded at the Tower, and Queen Elizabeth was once imprisoned here.

Important prisoners are executed on Tower Green, in front of St Peter's Church.

The royal armoury was established by Henry VIII. It contains all the latest weapons and armour.

The fierce lions are the most popular animals in the menagerie. Wooden lattices have been built to protect visitors.

The biggest draw to the Tower is the collection of wild animals in the royal menagerie. The tiger, wolf, porcupine and two lions kept in the Tower are not native to the country, and are therefore a great curiosity for Londoners and visitors alike.

Surrounded by a moat, the outer part of the Tower's complex contains soldiers' quarters, St Peter's Church and gardens. However, you will need special permission to enter the inner courtyard and the 11th-century White Tower.

London Bridge

The world-famous London Bridge is the only bridge crossing the River Thames and is a "must-see" for visitors. Built on 20 stone arches, it is so crowded with shops, chapels and houses that it looks more like a street than a bridge.

Sightseers' tip There is a wide variety of shops on London Bridge, but it is especially noted for the manufacture and retail of dress pins. There are usually crowds of people around the bridge's narrow stalls.

The roadway through the bridge is scarcely wider than a single cart and collisions are quite common. The buildings overhang the roadway so much that it is always gloomy, even during daylight.

A victim of the Reformation, St Thomas' Chapel at the centre of the bridge is now a grocer's shop.

Shops are so crammed together that only a passage 3.6 metres wide is left for traffic.

Water often rushes through the bridge's arches, creating a very loud roar.

The bridge slows down the river current, causing the Thames to freeze in cold weather. Frost fairs, with sports and games, are sometimes organized on the ice.

The bridge's massive piers force the tide of the Thames to bank up. This often causes a torrential flow through the arches, making it very dangerous to travel under the bridge by boat – a bit like shooting the rapids! The phenomenon has even given rise to a local proverb: "London Bridge was made for wise men to walk over and fools to go under".

Londoners flock to public executions and are completely at ease with the sight of bloody heads on poles.

At either end of London Bridge stand imposing gate towers. The squeamish are advised not to look up when approaching the gate at the southern end. Impaled on poles over the tower are the shrivelled heads of those executed for high treason!

The royal court

Now that Queen Elizabeth is in her sixties, the royal court is not as lively as it once was. However, if you manage to get an invitation you will be able to see at first hand the opulent lifestyles of the queen and her rich and powerful courtiers.

Hunting is a very popular royal sport. Queen Elizabeth owns several deer parks where she hunts the stag with her courtiers and important foreign visitors.

The court moves between several royal residences including the palaces of Greenwich (pictured above) and Richmond, Hampton Court and Nonsuch.

In summer the royal court travels around the country, staying in the homes of nobles.

When the court moves to a new palace, furniture, tapestries and treasures are taken with them.

If you wish to attend court and see the queen you will need a pass from the Lord Chamberlain.

Make sure you visit Westminster Abbey, the magnificent medieval church to the west of London. As well as containing many royal tombs, it also houses the coronation chair on which kings and queens are crowned.

The royal court is the centre of government in England. Queen Elizabeth is a very skilful ruler and has surrounded herself with faithful admirers. She uses social occasions to discuss important matters with her advisors or foreign visitors.

Sightseers' tip

In the evenings the royal court enjoys dancing. The most popular dance is called the volta. Men and women dance together. The man clasps the woman around the waist and lifts her in the air.

Survival guide

During Elizabeth's long reign, England has remained a peaceful and prosperous country. London has grown rapidly, and visitors will find it a very lively and exciting city. However, the increase in population means that outbreaks of plague and disease are common, and crime is rife.

Administration

Queen Elizabeth, with advice from her officials, decides foreign policy and internal legislation. If she needs to raise taxes or pass new laws she calls a parliament, although during her long reign she has called very few. The city of London is governed by a lord mayor and aldermen, who meet regularly at the Guildhall. The aldermen are usually powerful merchants and are elected from London's 26 wards. They select one of their number to be lord mayor.

Prices have risen throughout Elizabeth's reign. Currency includes gold sovereigns (one pound), angels (ten shillings) and silver crowns (five shillings).

Health

The streets of London are filthy and there are rats and other vermin everywhere. Illness and diseases such as smallpox, cholera and measles are also very common.

No-one yet knows what causes the frequent outbreaks of bubonic plague, although many think it is a divine punishment from God. Sneezing is an early symptom of the plague, and death usually follows within five days. To ward off the disease, doctors recommend that you carry a garland of herbs.

Most people die young. Only one person in ten reaches the age of 40.

There is a great number of beggars. Some pretend to be injured so people will give them more money.

Town criers announce forthcoming events, new laws and plague warnings.

Law and order

Although there is no paid police force, criminals who are caught face severe punishments. Penalties for petty crimes include a spell in the pillory, stocks or ducking stool. Or you could even have your face branded, your ears clipped or your nose slit!

While common people are hanged, nobles face the block and axe. However, the axe is rarely sharp enough to sever the head in one stroke.

Those accused of witchcraft are plunged into water. If they drown they are innocent, but if they survive they are deemed to be a witch and are executed. Ducking stools are also used to punish nagging wives who refuse to obey their husbands. Theft, riot, treason and murder are punishable by death.

People who commit minor crimes face the humiliation of a spell in the pillory or stocks. Criminals are incarcerated in a public place and passers-by throw rotten food at them.

❓Souvenir quiz

Take your time exploring Shakespeare's London. It is a fascinating city with plenty to see and experience. Before you leave, test your knowledge with this fun quiz. You will find the answers on page 32.

1. Coins are minted at only one place in England. Where is it?

a) The Royal Exchange – the trading and banking heart of the city.

b) The Tower of London – where the royal armoury and the crown jewels are kept.

c) The Guildhall – where the lord mayor and aldermen meet.

2. Shops and businesses in London are strictly regulated. What do you have to do before you can open a shop or practise a craft?

a) Serve a seven-year apprenticeship and pay a fee to join the appropriate guild.

b) Write to the queen asking for royal permission.

c) Pay the lord mayor five gold sovereigns.

3. Why should you avoid standing underneath hanging street signs?

a) They are not always securely fastened and can sometimes fall down.

b) Superstitious Londoners believe it will give you seven years' bad luck.

c) Shopkeepers do not like people loitering outside their shops.

4. Why do the authorities frown upon the playing of football?

a) They only sanction board games such as chess.

b) Leisure time should be used for archery practice.

c) It is a frequent cause of riot and bloodshed.

5. Punishments in Elizabethan London are very severe. How are nagging wives who refuse to obey their husbands punished?

a) Their ears are clipped and their faces branded with a hot iron.

b) They are executed.

c) They are put on a ducking stool and plunged into water.

6. What is a "wherry"?

a) A small boat used as a river taxi.

b) One of London Bridge's 20 stone arches.

c) A hawker who sells fruit during theatre performances.

7. Londoners enjoy bloodthirsty sports. What happens in bear-baiting?

a) Bears are hunted in the woods outside the city.

b) Fierce dogs are set on a tethered bear.

c) Bears are chased through the streets by children.

8. St Paul's central aisle is usually crowded with people chatting and doing business. What is its nickname?

a) It is known as Cathedral Close.

b) It is called Paul's Progress.

c) It is known as Paul's Walk.

9. Why do Londoners consider it fashionable to blacken their front teeth?

a) It contrasts well with their painted white faces.

b) Because the queen has no front teeth.

c) It disguises genuinely rotten teeth.

10. At which theatre is William Shakespeare an actor and a playwright?

a) The Globe.

b) The Swan.

c) The Rose.

31

Index

Acknowledgements

The consultant
Nicholas Robins works at Shakespeare's Globe theatre in London and is editor of its quarterly magazine, *Around the Globe.*

Inklink Firenze illustrators
Simone Boni, Alessandro Rabatti, Lorenzo Pieri, Luigi Critone, Lucia Mattioli, Francisco Petracchi, Theo Caneschi.

Additional illustrations
Vanessa Card, Jason Lewis, Nicki Palin.

Picture credits
b = bottom, c = centre, l = left, r = right, t = top
p.4 tr Burghley House Collection, Lincolnshire, UK/Bridgeman Art Library, London/New York; p.5 cr O'Shea Gallery,

London/Bridgeman Art Library, London/New York; p.9 tl In the collection of the Duke of Buccleuch & Queensberry, KT, cr Asprey & Co., London/Bridgeman Art Library, London/New York, br Burghley House Collection, Lincolnshire/Bridgeman Art Library, London/New York; p.11 br Museum of London Archaeological Service; p.12 tl Christies Images; p.16 tl AKG London; p.18 tr Mary Rose Trust; p.20 cl Dean and Chapter of Westminster; p.22 tl The Board of Trustees of the Armouries, (II.8); p.25 tl Fulgoni Photography; p.26 bl National Trust Photographic Library; p.27 tr Courtesy of the Dean and Chapter of Westminster/Angelo Hornak; p.28 bl ET Archive/British Museum

Every effort has been made to trace the copyright holders of the photographs. The publishers apologise for any inconvenience caused.

Souvenir quiz answers

1 = b) 2 = a) 3 = a) 4 = c) 5 = c) 6 = a) 7 = b) 8 = c) 9 = c) 10 = a)

This book is set in the year 1599.